Karl Jenkins

Requiem

D0933355

complete vocal score

SATB and piano

Boosey & Hawkes Music Publishers Ltd
www.boosey.com

Published by Boosey & Hawkes Music Publishers Ltd
Aldwych House
71–91 Aldwych
London
WC2B 4HN

www.boosey.com

 AN IMAGEM COMPANY

© Copyright 2005 by Boosey & Hawkes Music Publishers Ltd

ISMN 979-0-060-11684-1
ISBN 978-0-85162-485-3

Fifth impression 2011, with corrections. Seventh impression 2015, with corrections.

Printed by Halstan:
Halstan UK, 2–10 Plantation Road, Amersham, Bucks, HP6 6HJ. United Kingdom
Halstan DE, Weißliliengasse 4, 55116 Mainz. Germany

Music setting by Andrew Jones
Project management by Artemis Music Ltd

Original CD design by Paul Mitchell. Image courtesy of Warner Classics www.warnerclassics.com
Karl Jenkins photographed by Mitch Jenkins

Contents

1. Introit..1
2. Dies irae...11
3. The snow of yesterday..........................36
4. Rex tremendae......................................39
5. Confutatis..48
6. From deep in my heart........................ 53
7. Lacrimosa...56
8. Now as a spirit......................................65
9. Pie Jesu.. 70
10. Having seen the moon..........................75
11. Lux aeterna... 80
12. Farewell..88
13. In paradisum..93

Requiem is available on EMI Classics, catalogue numbers:
        7243 5 57966 2 2 CD
        7243 5 57966 5 3 Digital download

The CD, conducted by Karl Jenkins, features the choirs Serendipity (choral trainer — Timothy Rhys-Evans), Côr Caerdydd & Cytgan (choral trainer — Gwawr Owen) directed by Timothy Rhys-Evans and the West Kazakhstan Philharmonic Orchestra (Leader — Marat Bisengaliev) with Nicole Tibbels (soprano) and Clive Bell (shakuhachi).

The CD also features a recording of *In These Stones Horizons Sing* performed by Bryn Terfel (bass-baritone), Catrin Finch (harp) and Nigel Hitchcock (soprano saxophone).

For further information, visit www.emiclassics.com or www.karljenkins.com.

COMPOSER'S NOTE

Requiem

A Requiem is a Mass for the souls of the dead. In general, I have set the usual Latin movements but, in keeping with my usual trait of drawing from other cultures, I have also set five Japanese haiku 'death' poems. Such poems are usually to do with nature, have a single idea, and consist of seventeen syllables divided 5-7-5 over three lines. As one can see from the text, the Japanese view nature's water cycle (precipitation) as being synonymous with life.

I have combined the Western and Eastern texts in two of the haiku movements, Having Seen The Moon and Farewell, which incorporate the Benedictus and the Agnus Dei respectively. Both are intoned by male voices in a monastic style as a counterpoint to the Japanese text sung by females.

The instrumentation of these haiku settings includes the ancient Japanese wind instrument the shakuhachi. Elsewhere, as usual, I have used some ethnic drums (*eg* Arabic darabuca, Japanese daiko, frame drums) and even a hip-hop rhythm in the Dies irae!

The work is dedicated to my late father, a musician and an inspiration.

Karl Jenkins

Pronunciation guide

The vowels used in the Japanese texts should be sung as follows:

a	=	[a]
e	=	halfway between [ɛ] and [e] ('è' / 'é')
i	=	[i]
o	=	[ɔ]
u	=	halfway between [œ] and [y] ('er' / 'ü')

Instrumentation

Shakuhachi (or flute)
2 Horns in F
Timpani
*Percussion (3)
Harp
Strings

*1: glockenspiel, bamboo chimes, tubular bell (lowest possible A),
surdo, darabuca, hi-hat/side drum
2: mark tree, tambourine, cymbals, suspended cymbal/2 low floor tom-toms
3: triangle, rainstick, bass drum, 2 tam-tams

Note. The piano reduction in this vocal score is intended for rehearsal purposes only.

Performance materials available on hire

Duration: 55 minutes

in memoriam JDJ

REQUIEM
1. Introit

KARL JENKINS

for rehearsal only

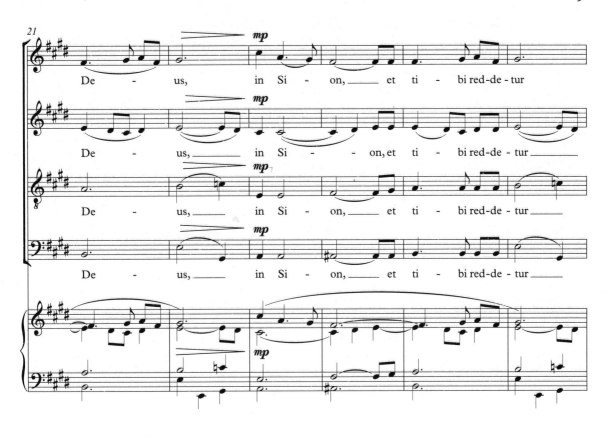

2. Dies irae

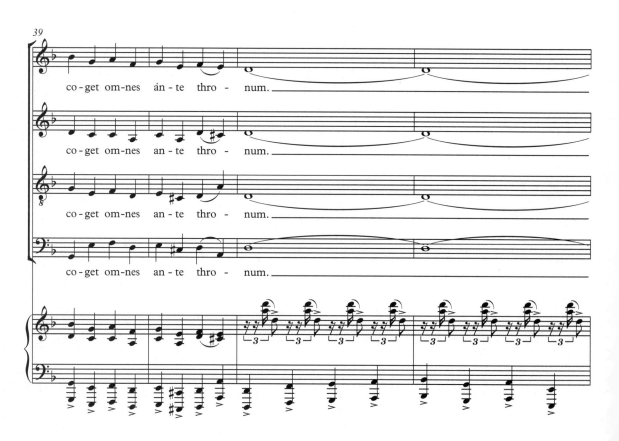

18

F

an - te thro - num.

an - te thro - num.

an - te thro - num.

an - te thro - num.

28

3. The snow of yesterday

that fell like cherry blossoms is water once again

Hana to mishi
Yuki wa kinouzo
Moto no mizu

Haiku by Gozan

Ha-na to mi-shi Yu-ki wa ki-no-u-zo Mo-to no mi - zu.

Mo-to no mi - zu. Mo-to no mi - zu.

rall.

4. Rex tremendae

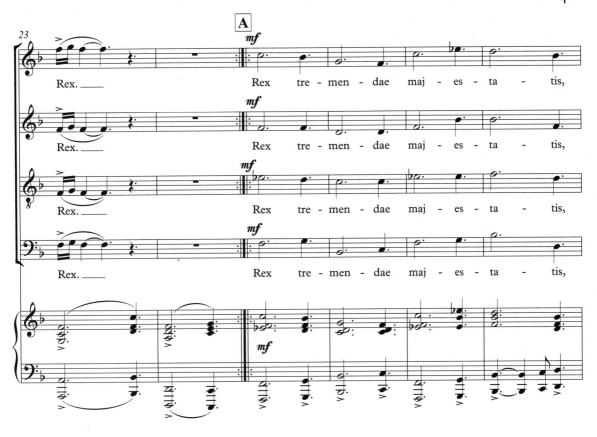

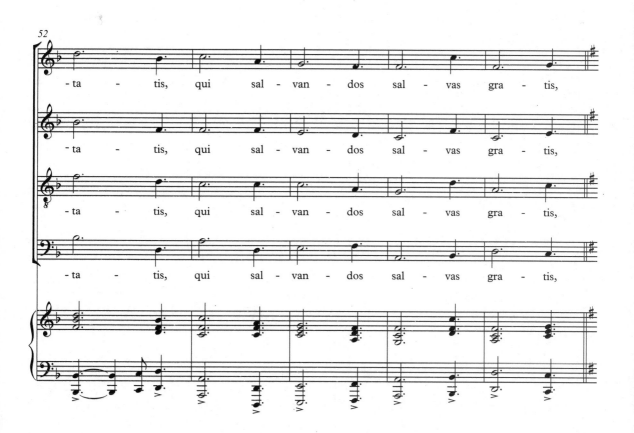

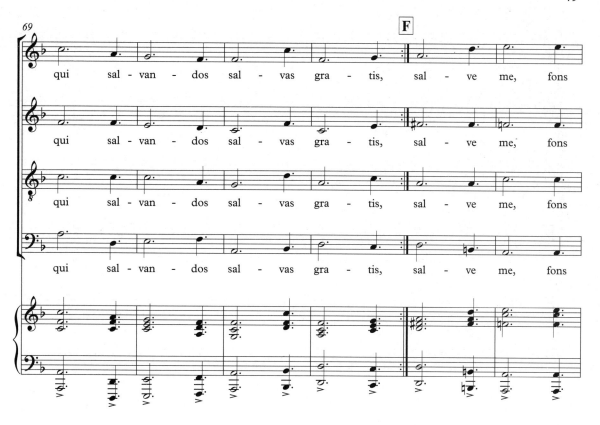

qui sal - van - dos sal - vas gra - tis, sal - ve me, fons

pi - e - ta - tis.

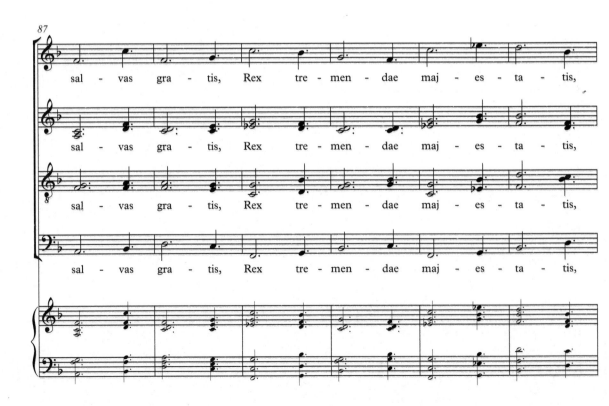

attacca

5. Confutatis

6. From deep in my heart

how beautiful are the snow clouds in the west

Kokoro kara
Yuki utsukushi ya
Nishi no kumo

Haiku by Issho

7. Lacrimosa

58

64

* This section (to bar 87) may be sung by two solo voices.

8. Now as a spirit

I shall roam the summer fields

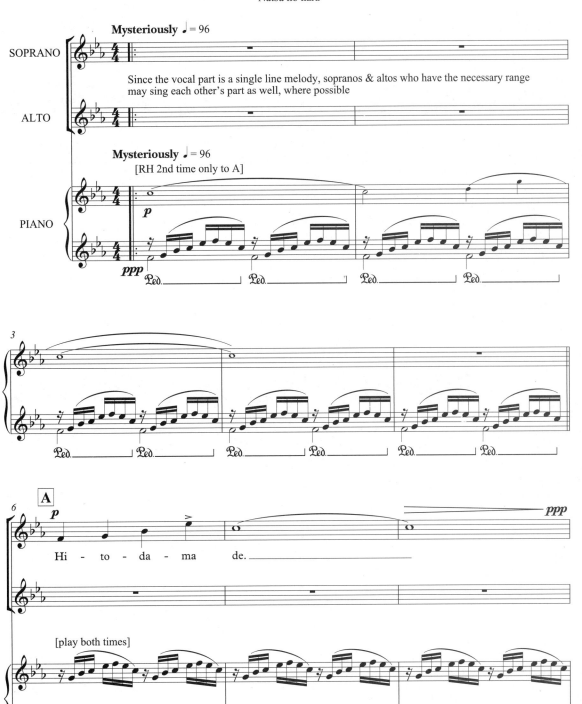

Haiku by Hokusai

Hitodama de
Yukuki sanjiya
Natsu no hara

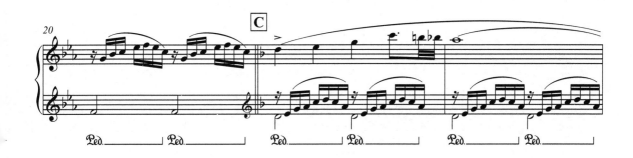

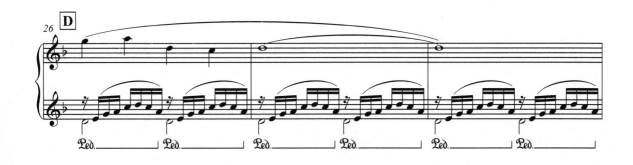

ha - ra.

molto dim. al niente

9. Pie Jesu

re - - qui - em. _____

re - - qui - em.

re - - qui - em.

re - - qui - em.

re - - qui - em.

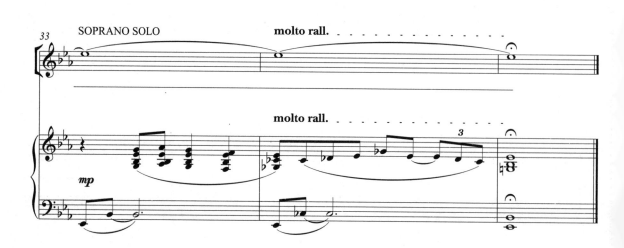

SOPRANO SOLO

molto rall. . . . .

molto rall. . . . .

10. Having seen the moon

even I take leave of this life with a blessing

Haiku by Kaga-no-Chiyo

Tsuki mo mite
Ware wa konoyowo
Kashiku kana

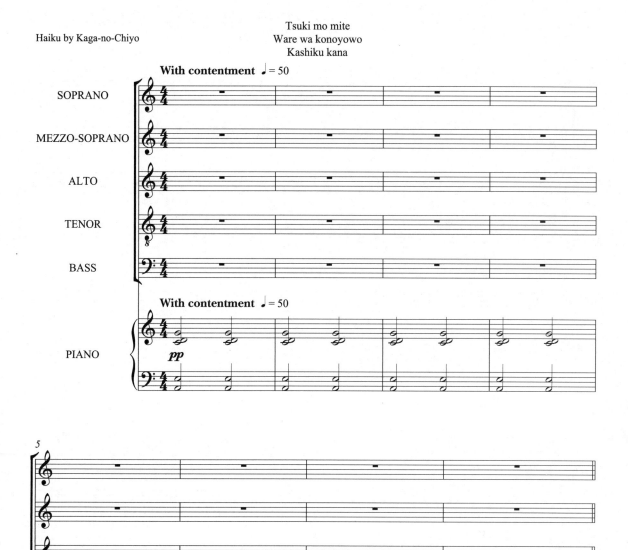

* At conductor's discretion Basses may sing an octave lower in bars 5–17 and in bars 29–40.

11. Lux aeterna

12. Farewell

I pass as do all things like dew on the grass

Haiku by Banzan

Mame de iyo
Miwa nara washino
Kusa no tsuyu

13. In paradisum

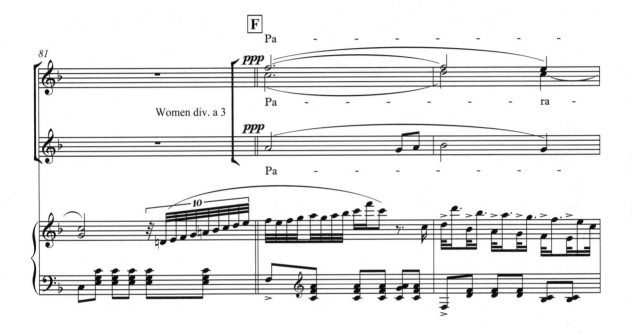

Works for chorus & orchestra
by Karl Jenkins

Stabat Mater
Vocal score (Contralto solo, SATB & piano)
ISMN: 979-0-060-11952-1

Gloria
Vocal score (Solo voice, SATB & piano)
ISMN: 979-0-060-12083-1

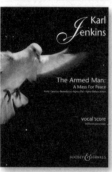

The Armed Man: A Mass for Peace
Complete full score
ISMN: 979-0-060-12255-2
Complete vocal score (SATB & piano)
ISMN: 979-0-060-11545-5
Choral suite vocal score (SATB & piano)
ISMN: 979-0-060-11410-6

Requiem
Vocal score (SATB & piano)
ISMN: 979-0-060-11684-1
Available separately:
Pie Jesu (SATB & piano)
ISMN: 979-0-060-11883-8
Pie Jesu (SSA & piano)
ISMN: 979-0-060-11887-6
Farewell
ISMN: 979-0-060-11886-9
Three Haikus (SATB & piano)
ISMN: 979-0-060-11888-3

Te Deum
Vocal score (SATB & piano)
ISMN: 979-0-060-12031-2

The Peacemakers
Vocal score (SATB & piano)
ISMN: 979-0-060-12434-1

Joy to the World
Vocal score (SATB & piano)
ISMN: 979-0-060-12217-0

Stella natalis
Vocal score (SATB & piano)
ISMN: 979-0-060-12216-3